POETRY
MARCHING
FOR SINDY

VIRGINIA PESEMAPEO BORDELEAU

POETRY
MARCHING
FOR SINDY

TRANSLATED BY
SUSAN OURIOU

INANNA poetry & fiction

Toronto, Ontario, Canada
www.inanna.ca

The publisher gratefully acknowledges the support of the Canada Council for the Arts and the Ontario Arts Council. The publisher is also grateful for the financial assistance received from the Government of Canada.

Cover design: Meg Bowen
Original cover artwork: Staifany Gonthier

Library and Archives Canada Cataloguing in Publication

Title: Poetry marching for Sindy / Virginia Pesemapeo Bordeleau ; translated by Susan Ouriou.
Other titles: Poésie en marche pour Sindy. English
Names: Pesemapeo Bordeleau, Virginia, 1951- author. | Ouriou, Susan, translator.
Description: Translation of: Poésie en marche pour Sindy. | In English, translated from the French.
Identifiers: Canadiana (print) 20240360060 | Canadiana (ebook) 20240360095 | ISBN 9781771339742
  (softcover) | ISBN 9781771339759 (EPUB) | ISBN 9781771339766 (PDF)
Subjects: LCGFT: Poetry.
Classification: LCC PS8631.E797 P6413 2024 | DDC C841/.6—dc23

Printed and bound in Canada

Inanna Publications and Education Inc.
210 Founders College, York University
4700 Keele Street, Toronto, Ontario M3J 1P3 Canada
Telephone: (416) 736-5356 Fax: (416) 736-5765
Email: inanna.publications@inanna.ca Website: www.inanna.ca

For Sindy's family

Powerful are the shadows
That haunt us

Shooting stars in orbits of anarchy
Sparks of madness
Buffeted by blasts of hatred

I paint totems
In a palette of fire
Torches to guide you

Your life laid down in a forest of ferns
Perhaps in the hollow of a path

You will return
For no one can travel without coming back

You will be no more in family photos
A blank space in the picture
Your finger pointing
At the imperceptible
During our hours of insomnia
Sleep beyond reach
Aimed at the night sky
The silent request
Where are you   Sindy

On occasion sorrow engulfs us
Storms of rage leave us shaken
Force us to see our lack of clairvoyance
When was it that you succumbed
To your hope in him and his promises

Did he speak to you of love

There has never been a mystery
To the fragility we feel
Confronted with glances of indifference

The habit of silence

But the courage of those who love you
Knows no boundaries

You will never be a grandmother
So   be beautiful   be immutable
You   gentle to the core
And draw from the love of your family
The strength to bear the flame
In the darkness of the world

Tell us your secret
Tell us your truth
Through the rustling of leaves
Through the lapping of waves
In the sighing of winds

Red women
We are the word rising from deep in the loins
From wombs   where we bear the weight of humanity
We are the voices to call your name
Sindy

It will never be too late
Woman sacrificed
For you to appear to us
Far above the land
Standing   you   alone
Shrouded by the fog of human stupidity

You   our Mother   the earth
Fed by the sorrows
Of the mothers and the fathers
Whose daughters devoured by silence
Seek the light
Yet they were fertile ground for life
Tell us   why are we so afraid

Sindy   you keep your distance still
But we long for your presence
The ceremonies await you
The Way of the Ancestors too
The drums sound
Within reach of your spirit

The days without you multiply
Yet even should they turn to centuries
Your loved ones will continue to search for you beyond death
For no sorrow holds
As much power
As the loss of a child

Mother Earth will whisper from her womb
Your name written on her skin
Not tattooed there
But emerging from within
Like an animal's fur

Flowers and moss will say
That you live on
In the heart of your mother   of your father
Of all those who have loved you

We will write your name
In the places your spirit wanders
Abiding
Till the discovery of your body

Long is the winter
The wait for spring
With its sun burning
The carpet of snow
Shrouding the hope
Johnny and Émily hold onto

They search without reprieve
They who brought you into the world
Seek your scent
Hidden beneath moss
In the hollow of rocks
Or in the memory
Of those who wished to hurt you

Elf fairy sprite
Parents dream
Of the child to come
Imagine her body
Her being life-filled

Yours dream only of bones
Vestiges of their daughter

Your father's haunted gaze
Where suffering lies
Born of not knowing you are safe
Born of the inability to protect you

Your absence found in the pained silence
Of your mother

Your beauty wafts above
The crowns of trees
Clothed in clouds
Like the wedding dress of a young bride
Borne away on the day of her nuptials

We are sisters
Other than by blood
We are sisters
In that womanhood
The other half of the world
Crushes and kills

Yet are we not sacred bodies
Womb bodies bodies of forbearance
Why are we found guilty
For the life we give

Bodies of resource
Like dens for foxes
Whose beauty is blind
A habitat for new humans
Who shelter there
To invent a story   a life

It is no fairy tale
This knowing in advance that our tiny guest
Will depart   a violent leave-taking
It has always been thus
The oldest story of them all

Sindy   your spirit lives in us
Our thoughts gravid with your memory

The same is true of our sisters
Both missing and murdered

We speak of you
Our words ride the wind
We call to your soul with all our strength
For your return
To your family of spirit and blood

We have marched in the streets
Red dresses
A river of blood unfurling across the asphalt
And the words borne by your mother and sister
Sindy   we will find you
Words kneaded in hope
Deep within the clan

Your mother said of you to me
She loved dogs
Helped those without shelter
Man or beast

Your father said to me
She was smart
Always wore fine clothes
Filled the house with her diplomas

The gentle timbre of their voices
Broken with emotion

Fragile daughter   have you witnessed
The meaning of all things
From eternity on
Universal knowledge

Or the time of cosmic dust behind us
Leaking from the holes
In our primate consciousness

Do you hear the sound of nascent springs
One ear glued to the belly of stones
Do you hear the changing timbre of winds
Caressed by the sparkle of the polar star
Overhead   farther than the edge of the world

Do you share the memory of the ancestors
With the lichen as it waits for the caribou
Your cheek laid on the roughness of its skin

Are you cold   do you feel alone   solar daughter

I will not speak to you of crows
Whose black eyes know
See beyond primal waters
Witness the motion all around you

Yet I can tell you
What your father and your mother
Feel in the secret of their silence
I know the words
To raise the veil on the indescribable

I won't tell you of a son   my own
Marred by the rigid mask
The one your face wears now
Turned to the roots of flowers

What shall we say to the ancestors reaching out to us
We   blind parents
Who could not be walls of love
Thick enough to protect you
Who were not there when it mattered
To form a bulletproof vest   where it counted

The waters of our wombs
Ours the mothers
Are no longer made of original fluids
But of sand reddened by our wounds
Oceans of tears of brine
Salt on our lacerations

Lament   to what end
Lament   what exactly
Are we not the cause
Of all these ills

Fertile as we are

Often
We yearn to vanish into the dark
Into the night of non-existence
To no longer be   to no longer give life
Or signs thereof

To return to the beginning of that very first cell
Pregnant with all dreamed humanity
That seed of the earth
Our fertility
Find it and crush it underfoot

Do we know the rage of mothers
The rage of wombs that give without end

And the killers who explode
Decimating that life offering
Those creatures who murder their sisters   their brothers

Tell me   Sindy
Did he kill you like a fly
Of no worth   no importance
Without contempt even
For contempt begets respect
The way hatred is a sister to love

Did he dig a trench
In which to bury you   like shame denied
A red trail over the trodden grass
A sanctuary for your final slumber

Do we know that one day   perhaps
Wombs risk closing in on themselves
Do we know that the rage of mothers
Risks outweighing the love for giving
When mothers indeed kill their young
When madness spreads all around

To cry in the echoless desert
Emptied of what is left of the sky
Of what is left of fabricated promises
Never to be kept
Never realized
Never fulfilled
Is no better than crying to an assembly of ghosts

How many cries will have to be buried
In the humus of our Ancient Mother
For our daughters to return to us at last

Killing the mothers to kill the child-to-be
Do you hear Sindy   the silence of the tikinagans

Cradleboards in which no infant babbles

Women go astray there
Wander off and turn away
Call for help
Search for the path
Yet so close at hand

We know what it is to be lost
As familiar as our breasts engorged with milk
Return to slumber   Sindy
One day your sisters' wrath will awaken you

Your sisters   insurgent women

Will you flower   one day
In ephemeral springtimes
Amid the blackened feet of bulrushes
Will you rise from the marsh
Like a plant devouring sorrow
That of your mother
That of your father

Your bones threaded like seashells
Will they rise from creeks
From lakes   no matter how deep
Is that miracle possible

I call on the heart of earthly creatures
On the spirit of the roots that push at your hands
And imprison your vertebrae
In their tough embrace

I call on the spirits of the forests
Breath held as I wait
For them to deliver you at last
Beneath the watch of the silent moon
Fingers of soft light
Laid on your temples

Again the wind has torn away the curtain of leaves
Baring the landscape   exposing the horizon
And the skeleton of trees

Again white death
Prowls round the yard
Poised for its moment to sweep within
Once more   you will be a frozen island
Lost in the twilight of time

Listen to the murmur   my sister
Welling up from women's voices
Those subterranean voices close by
Listen and heed the call
Follow the narrow gap of daylight
That speaks to you of return

All mornings are born here
They slide in on the silk of dawn
Latch onto the sighs of forests in November
That month when we cease to hope

Watch the passing of the clouds
Like vaporous boats
Over a silence none can hear
But you   nestled perhaps within a swamp
Shelter for the jut of your bones

The essence of all matter
Hinges on nothing at times
A perfect intuition that crosses
the slumbering room

A rustling of leaves
Amid the motion of planets
That tears sleep asunder
As we look to the night for an answer
In a nightmare whose prey is you

The gods no longer listen to women
Nor see the tears salting their cheeks
Yet prayers travel unceasingly
From lips to unmoved cathedrals

We will pour the glass of red out on the path
Extract the firewater from our blood

The dance will not end with the drum
The jingles on regalia will chime and bounce
Your sisters will stamp on the ground
To tell you that they are alive
Spirited still despite the shadows lying in wait

So long as we dance
Death will bow down

Our feet caress the Mother Body
And drift across this country of exile
Whose flowers we are

I am wearied
By the time gone by
And the suffering here still
We will not claim that the salt of days
Can heal   or disinfect the hurt

Poetry   is words to console
Wind to carry our voices
A sound to mask the emptiness
This we know

ACKNOWLEDGEMENTS

Above all, I would like to thank Émily and Johnny Wylde, Sindy's parents. Thank you also to Jean-Guy Côté for his support and his patience.

Credit: Christian Leduc

Born in Jamésie in north-west Quebec, Virginia Pesemapeo Bordeleau is a multidisciplinary eeyou artist. For the past forty-four years, she has exhibited in Quebec, Canada, Europe and Mexico. In 2006, she was awarded the regional prix d'excellence by the Conseil des arts et lettres du Québec and earned Télé-Québec's distinction for poetry. In 2012, she was the winner of the Abitibi-Témiscamingue literary award. Since 2007, she has published three novels, three collections of poetry, one storybook, one artist's book and a collection of correspondence. In 2020, she was granted Abitibi-Témiscamingue's artist of the year award by the Conseil des arts et lettres du Québec. A retrospective exhibition of her forty-year career was also held at MA, Rouyn-Noranda's art museum. In 2021, she was awarded a medal by Québec's Assemblée nationale du Québec for her life's work and in 2023 she was appointed as Chevalier in the Ordre des Palmes académiques. In 2024, the

Université de Moncton granted her an honorary Doctor of Arts. Virginia still lives in Abitibi-Témiscamingue where she continues to paint, sculpt and, of course, write with the authenticity that characterizes all of her work.

Susan Ouriou is an award-winning literary translator, fiction writer and conference interpreter. Her most recent translation of Virginia Pesemapeo Bordeleau's writing, *The Lover, the Lake*, was short-listed for the 2021 Governor General's translation award. Her translations *Kukum* by Michel Jean and *White Resin* by Emmanuelle Walter were also short-listed for the GG in 2023 and 2022 respectively. An earlier translation, *Pieces of Me* by Charlotte Gingras, won that same award. With Christelle Morelli, Susan also co-translated Virginia Pesemapeo Bordeleau's *Winter Child* and *Blue Bear Woman*. As well, she and Christelle Morelli co-translated Emmanuelle Walter's *Stolen Sisters: The Story of Two Missing Girls, Their Families and How Canada Has Failed Indigenous Women*, another GG translation award short-listing. In 2023, she published and performed *Many Mothers, Seven Skies – Scenes for Tomorrow* with the Many Mothers collective. Most recently, in 2024 Susan Ouriou's translation *The Future* of Catherine Leroux's novel *L'Avenir* was the winner of Canada Reads. She lives in Calgary, Alberta.